DU

Volcanoes

BY CHRISTY STEELE

Steadwell Books

Raintree Steck-Vaughn Publishers

A Harcourt Company

Austin · New York

www.steck-vaughn.com

Nature on the Rampage

Published by Raintree Steck-Vaughn Publishers, an imprint of Steck-Vaughn Company.
Library of Congress Cataloging-in-Publication Data
Steele, Christy.
    Volcanoes/by Christy Steele.
        p.cm.--(Nature on the rampage)
    Includes index.
    Summary: Explains how volcanoes form and what effects they have on the environment.
    ISBN 0-7398-1796-5
    1. Volcanoes--Juvenile literature. [1. Volcanoes.] I. Title. II. Series.
QE521.3 .S73 2000
363.34'95--dc21

                                                99-058671

Printed in the United States of America
10 9 8 7 6 5 4 3 2 1 LB 02 01 00 99

Produced by Compass Books
Photo Acknowledgments
Dembinsky Photo Associates/S. Jonasson, 27
Digital Stock, cover, title page, 4, 6, 10, 13, 16, 26, 29
Photo Network, 19, 20–21
Visuals Unlimited/Jim Hughes, 15; Peter Ziminski, 23

Content Consultant:
The author wishes to thank the staff at the Cascades Volcano Observatory for their help with this book.

CONTENTS

What Volcanoes Are 5

Volcano Eruptions 11

Volcanoes in History 17

Volcanoes and Science 25

Glossary 30

Addresses and Internet Sites 31

Index 32

What Volcanoes Are

A volcano is an opening in Earth's surface that connects to an underground magma source. Magma is melted rock inside Earth. Magma breaks through Earth's crust and forms volcanoes. The crust is the outer layer of Earth.

Different kinds of volcanoes have different volcanic forms. The form is the part of the volcano that people can see. Some volcanoes look like large mountains. Others look like small hills. Some look like holes in the ground.

Volcanoes erupt. An eruption happens when something bursts through a volcano's opening. Volcanoes can erupt rocks, ash, hot gas, or lava. Lava is magma rock that has reached the surface.

Lava can pile up and harden after an eruption. This builds a mountain around the volcano's opening.

Layers of Earth

Earth is made up of three layers. The core is the center of Earth. It is made of very hot, heavy rock and metal. The mantle is the middle layer of Earth. It too is made of rock. Parts of the mantle melt and make magma. The crust is the thin, outer layer of Earth. It is cooler and made of light rocks. If Earth were an egg, the crust would be about as thick as an eggshell.

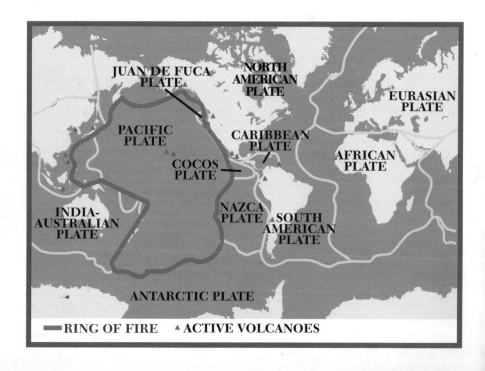

Where Volcanoes Form

Volcanoes are found on land or under water. They start at cracks or weak places on the crust. Some parts of the crust are thinner than others. The thin parts of the crust can be weak.

Other weak places occur because of Earth's plates. A plate is a giant piece of Earth's crust. Scientists believe many plates fit together like puzzle pieces to make up Earth's crust.

Plates move. They slide over magma in the mantle. The plates' movements may make cracks in the crust. Most cracks happen where two moving plates meet each other.

The Pacific Plate moves past many other plates. This plate's movements have caused most of the world's volcanoes to form around its edges. People call the edges of the Pacific Plate the Ring of Fire because of its many volcanoes.

This diagram shows the main plates that make up Earth's crust. Volcanoes often start at plate edges.

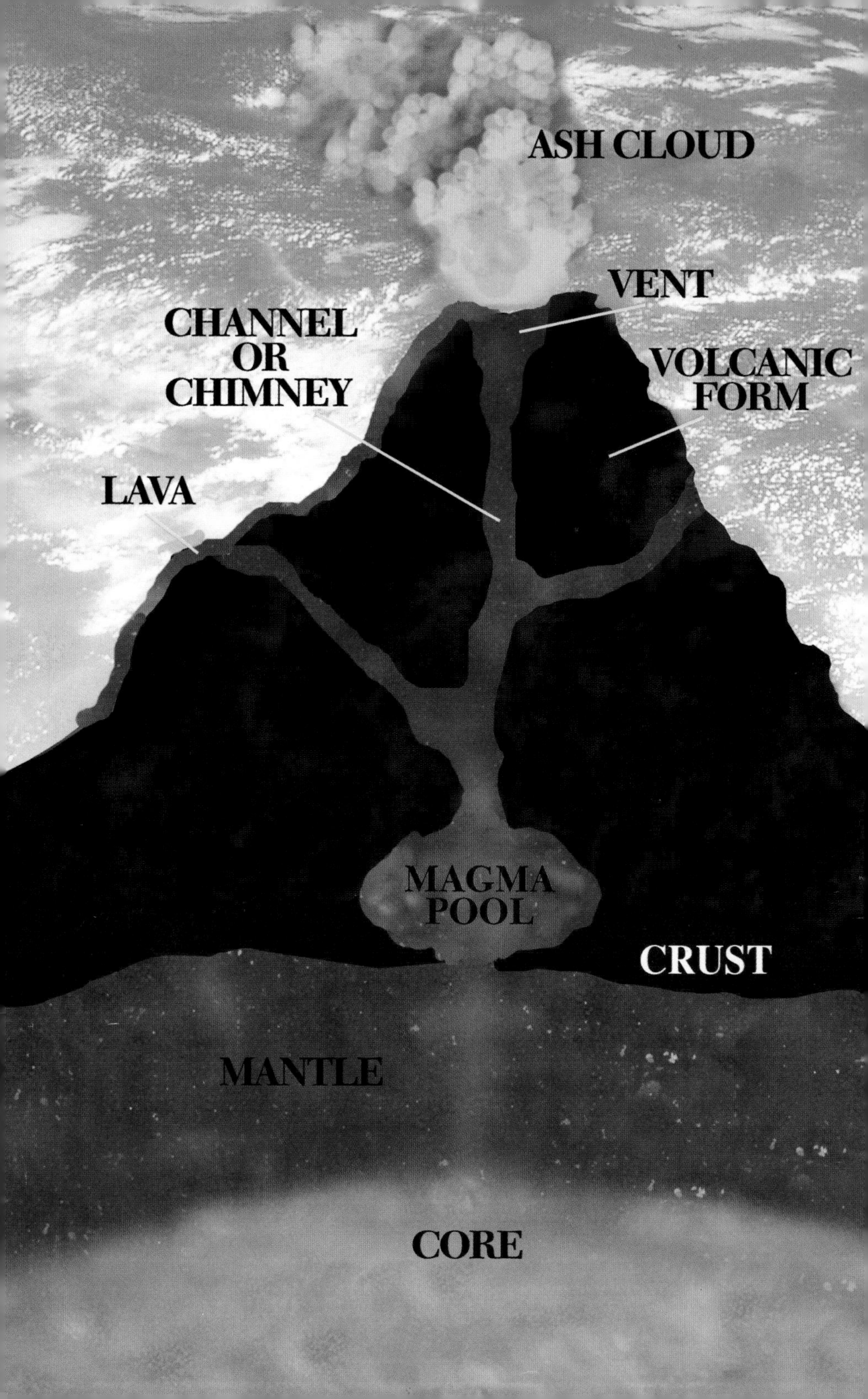

ASH CLOUD

VENT

CHANNEL
OR
CHIMNEY

VOLCANIC
FORM

LAVA

MAGMA
POOL

CRUST

MANTLE

CORE

Parts of a Volcano

Every volcano must have a source of magma. Magma is lighter than solid rock. It rises from the mantle and flows toward Earth's surface. Magma sometimes collects under the surface in a pool. A volcano may have several of these magma pools.

Another part of a volcano is its channel, or chimney. A channel is a pipelike tunnel that goes from the mantle to the crust's surface. Magma flows up from the mantle through the channel. A volcano may have many channels.

A vent is the opening at the top of a volcano's channel. The vent opens to Earth's surface.

Eruptions create the volcanic form. During eruptions, lava, gas, rock, and ash clouds can escape from the vent. Once magma reaches the vent, it is called lava. Over time, the lava hardens. The rocks, ash, and hard lava make a volcanic form around the vent.

The volcano's form changes after each eruption. New lava and ash may pile on top of the old material. This will make the form taller and thicker.

 This diagram shows the parts of a volcano.

VOLCANO ERUPTIONS

Several things can cause volcano eruptions. Plate movements may start eruptions. Sometimes earthquakes start eruptions. An earthquake is the sudden shaking of Earth's crust. Earthquakes can open new cracks in the crust. Lava then can erupt through the new cracks.

Volcanoes have different kinds of eruptions. Hot steam and gases such as carbon dioxide, sulfur dioxide, and hydrogen escape during small eruptions. Other eruptions release large clouds of ash and these gases. During some eruptions, lava spits from cracks and forms lava streams. Lava, ash, gas, and rocks explode miles into the air during large eruptions.

This volcano in Hawaii is having a small eruption of hot steam and gases.

Volcano Flows

Huge streams of lava make up lava flows. Lava can be thick or thin. Thick lava moves slowly and does not travel far. People usually have time to move away from the path of a thick-lava flow. Thin lava covers large areas quickly. People often do not have time to escape from a thin-lava flow.

Lava flows can burn or bury everything in their paths. Since 1983, lava flows in Hawaii have buried more than 200 houses.

A pyroclastic flow is a mixture of hot gas, ash, and stones. Pyroclastic flows are fast and deadly. They are around 1,500° Fahrenheit (815° C). They rush down volcanoes at speeds up to 150 miles (241 km) per hour. These flows destroy anything in their paths.

Heavy rain or melting snow and ice can start mudflows. These flows are made of mud, rock, and water. Mudflows travel up to 40 miles (64 km) an hour. They can spread out over a 50-mile (80-km) area.

This lava flow in Hawaii has buried everything in its path. The top of the flow has cooled and hardened.

Kinds of Volcano Damage

Small eruptions do little harm. The escaped steam and gas simply mix with the air. But large eruptions can cause serious harm and create damaging flows.

Great amounts of ash escape into the air during large eruptions. Wind can blow clouds of ash far from erupting volcanoes. Since 1983, about 80 airplanes have been damaged by flying into ash clouds. Huge ash clouds also can change the weather by blocking some of the sun's rays. Some large ash clouds can make the weather colder for a year or more. Colder weather may damage crops.

Falling ash can be heavy. It can cover roofs and make them fall down. This can crush people inside buildings. Falling ash can fill lakes. The water then mixes with the ash and turns to mud. All the fish and plants in the lake die.

During large eruptions, all sizes of rocks from the volcano explode into the air. Large falling rocks can kill people and animals.

Volcano flows cause much damage. Lava flows can start fires. Mudflows rip up trees and houses

 A pyroclastic flow destroyed this forest in Washington State.

and bury everything in their paths. Pyroclastic flows can destroy entire forests.

Volcano eruptions also can cause tsunamis. Tsunamis are huge waves that travel a long way over oceans. They cause great floods when they wash over land.

VOLCANOES IN HISTORY

The name volcano comes from the Roman god of fire. His name was Vulcan. Romans believed he lived underneath a mountain on a small island in the Mediterranean Sea. The mountain erupted fire. Romans named the island Vulcano. Today, all mountains that erupt are called volcanoes after the god Vulcan.

People on the Hawaiian Islands believed the goddess Pele made volcanoes. Pele could change herself into lava. Pele stamped her feet or dug with her magic stick when she got mad. These actions made volcanoes erupt.

Scientists call smooth lava pahoehoe. This Hawaiian lava flow shows what hardening pahoehoe looks like.

Vesuvius Eruption in A.D. 79

Mount Vesuvius in Italy erupted on August 24 to 25 in the year A.D. 79. A huge cloud of ash rose into the sky. Vesuvius erupted ash clouds and started many pyroclastic flows.

Ash and stones fell on the nearby town of Pompeii. Stones made roofs and buildings fall down on people. Many people left the town. On August 25, Vesuvius erupted a cloud of ash and poisonous gas. It rushed through Pompeii. Everyone left in the town died.

Herculaneum was a small town near a different side of Mount Vesuvius. On August 25, a thick mudflow and a pyroclastic flow of hot ash, rock, and poisonous gas exploded from Vesuvius. The flows quickly buried Herculaneum under 65 feet (20 m) of rock and mud. Everyone left in Herculaneum died.

Tambora Eruption in 1815

On April 10, 1815, the Indonesian volcano Tambora erupted. The volcano spit rock and ash into the sky. Stones and ash fell on nearby cities. A pyroclastic flow ripped apart houses and uprooted trees.

About 92,000 people died. Some died in the eruption. Others died afterward from lack of

food. The eruption killed crops. Tambora was the deadliest eruption in recorded history.

Tambora's ash cloud made the weather around the world about 10 degrees colder than average during the following year. Many people called it "the year without a summer." It snowed in the eastern United States during June 1815. The cold weather killed many crops around the world.

▲ Mount Pelée is still an active volcano. It may erupt again someday.

Mount Pelée Eruption in 1902

Mount Pelée is a volcano on the island of Martinique in the Caribbean Sea. In February of 1902, smoke and ash poured out of Pelée. Animals tried to escape the volcano's ash. Ants, foot-long centipedes, and snakes invaded the nearby town of St. Pierre. About 50 people and around 200 animals died from insect and snake bites.

On May 8, 1902, Mount Pelée erupted a huge cloud of hot ash, steam, and poisonous gas. This pyroclastic flow moved quickly into St. Pierre. It blasted buildings and started fires. The hot gas and steam burned people's skin. People breathed in the poison gas and died.

About 30,000 people died. Only two people in St. Pierre lived through the eruption. One was a shoemaker living on the edge of the town away from the poisonous gases. The other man was a prisoner in an underground cell.

Mount Saint Helens Eruption in 1980

The serious study of volcanoes began after the Pelée eruption. This science is called volcanology. Volcanologists are scientists who study volcanoes.

Mount Saint Helens is a volcano in the state of Washington. For 123 years, the volcano was resting. On March 27, 1980, the volcano had a small eruption. It blew out steam and ash. Other small eruptions followed.

Volcanologists studied Mount Saint Helens. They looked at its ash and gas. Scientists saw that the volcano was growing 5 feet (2 m) each day. Volcanologists believed Saint Helens might have a large eruption. So they warned people near the volcano.

On May 18, 1980, an avalanche made Mount Saint Helens erupt. An avalanche is a large amount of snow, ice, or soil that falls down a mountain. The explosion blasted smoke, steam,

 A pyroclastic flow destroyed many places around Mount Saint Helens.

and ash into the sky. A pyroclastic flow carried ash, steam, and rocks for about 230 miles (370 km). It blew down trees and buildings.

The eruption killed 57 people. This eruption was the worst volcano disaster in North America.

VOLCANOES AND SCIENCE

About 500 active volcanoes exist around the world. An active volcano is a volcano that has erupted once in recorded history. The United States has 50 active volcanoes. Most of these are in Hawaii, Alaska, and Washington.

Volcanologists study these active volcanoes. They want to learn more about how volcanoes work. They also want to learn how to better predict when volcanoes will erupt. They then can warn people. Better warnings can help save people's lives.

Lava from a volcano in Hawaii is making steam as it flows into the ocean. Hawaii has many active volcanoes.

Volcano Safety

Today, scientists sometimes can tell if a volcano may erupt. Officials may issue a volcano warning. This means a volcano is about to erupt. People can save their lives by evacuating during volcano warnings. Evacuate means to leave quickly.

Sometimes volcanoes erupt without warning. People then should take shelter inside strong buildings with closed windows. This will protect them from some ash and gases. People should use wet cloths to cover their mouths and noses. Breathing or swallowing dust or ash can be deadly.

People should stay away from the ocean if a volcano erupts. An eruption could cause a flood or a tsunami. Tsunamis might wash over land.

Tools Volcanologists Use

Scientists have invented tools to study volcanoes. They wear special suits and hoods to protect them. These suits will not catch on fire. They wear heavy boots to protect their feet from heat.

Volcanologists put seismometers near a volcano. Seismometers help tell scientists when earthquakes happen. Earthquakes often come before a volcano erupts.

▲ **People have evacuated this area in Iceland because a volcano is erupting.**

Tiltmeters measure how much volcanoes grow. Volcanoes often grow before they erupt.

Volcanologists use thermometers to measure a volcano's temperature. Volcanoes get hotter before they erupt.

Good Uses for Volcanoes

Volcano eruptions are important tools for creating new crust. Lava hardens to form volcanic rock. Volcanic rock makes up most of Earth's crust. Large volcanoes rise up from ocean floors to start islands. Volcanoes created islands such as Hawaii and Iceland.

A volcano's hot water and steam give off heat. People in Iceland put pipes underground near hot lava flows. They pump water through the pipes to heat their homes.

Lava flows and volcanic ash add minerals to soil. These minerals help plants grow. Farmers raise crops near volcanoes.

Some people are trying to control lava flows. In Italy, the government bombed lava flows to change their paths. In Iceland, villagers sprayed lava flows with cold water to cool them and slow them down. People someday may learn new ways to lessen the damage from volcano eruptions.

This lava flow is hardening into black volcanic rock. Igneous rock is another name for volcanic rock.

GLOSSARY

channel (CHAN-uhl)—a pipelike opening through which magma flows up to a volcano's vent

core (CORE)—the center of Earth; very hot metals make up Earth's core.

crust (CRUHST)—the outer layer of Earth

lava (LAH-vuh)—melted rock that has escaped from a volcano to Earth's surface

magma (MAG-muh)—hot, melted rock under Earth

magma pool (MAG-muh POOL)—a huge pool of magma in Earth's mantle

mantle (MAN-tuhl)—the middle layer of Earth; thick, heavy rocks make up the mantle.

pahoehoe (puh-HO-ay-ho-ay)—a Polynesian word scientists use to describe the surface of smooth lava flows

vent (VENT)—the opening at the top of a volcano's channel; lava and gas erupt through the vent.

Hawaii Volcanoes National Park
P.O. Box 52
Hawaii National Park, HI 96718-0052

U.S. Geological Survey, MS977
345 Middlefield Road
Menlo Park, CA 94025

Cascades Volcano Observatory
http://vulcan.wr.usgs.gov

FEMA for Kids: The Disaster Area
http://www.fema.gov/kids/dizarea.htm

Volcano Lovers
http://whyfiles.news.wisc.edu/031volcano/index.
  html

Volcano World
http://volcano.und.nodak.edu/vw.html

INDEX

ash cloud, 9, 14, 19

channel, 9
core, 6
crust, 5, 6, 7, 9, 11, 28

earthquakes, 11, 26

floods, 15

Hawaii, 12, 17
Herculaneum, 18

lava, 5, 9, 11, 12, 17, 18
lava flow, 12, 14, 28

magma, 5, 6, 7, 9, 11
magma pool, 9
mantle, 6, 7, 9
Mount Saint Helens,
    22–23
Mount Vesuvius, 18
mudflow, 12, 14, 18

Pele, 17
plates, 7, 11
Pompeii, 18
pyroclastic flow, 12, 15,
    18, 21, 23

Ring of Fire, 7
Romans, 17

St. Pierre, 20–21
seismometer, 26

Tambora, 18–19
thermometer, 27
tiltmeter, 27
tsunami, 15, 26

vent, 9
volcanic rock, 28
volcano warning, 26
Vulcan, 17

Washington State, 22,
    25